World Famous
Indians

Vishwamitra Sharma

V&S PUBLISHERS

Published by:

V&S PUBLISHERS

F-2/16, Ansari Road, Daryaganj, New Delhi-110002
☎ 011-23240026, 011-23240027 • *Fax:* 011-23240028
Email: info@vspublishers.com • *Website:* www.vspublishers.com

Branch : Hyderabad
5-1-707/1, Brij Bhawan (Beside Central Bank of India Lane)
Bank Street, Koti, Hyderabad - 500 095
☎ 040-24737290
E-mail: vspublishershyd@gmail.com

Branch Office : Mumbai
Jaywant Industrial Estate, 2nd Floor–222, Tardeo Road
Opposite Sobo Central Mall, Mumbai – 400 034
☎ 022-23510736
E-mail: vspublishersmum@gmail.com

Follow us on: 🐦 f in

All books available at **www.vspublishers.com**

Printed at : Repro Knowledgecast Limited, Thane

Contents

Preface

Centuries of serfdom, strife and struggle followed, as we sought to assert our identity and preserve the nation's rich cultural heritage. It was during this period of enslavement that countless inspiring personalities came to the helm, exhorting countrymen to awake from their slumber, throw off the foreign yoke and reclaim India's rightful place among the comity of nations. Where a writer like Premchand used the written word as a source of inspiration.

Some of the most inspiring personalities lived during the 20th Century, a crucial period in the country's march towards independence. In this reawakening, individuals from every sphere contributed their mite: writers, artists and philosophers – even film and sports personalities. For instance, hockey wizard Dhyan Chand helped India whitewash all the white, supposedly superior nations during the Amsterdam (1928), Los Angeles (1932) and Berlin (1936) Olympics. India's stupendous gold run during this period dazzled onlookers, stunned opponents and silenced critics. It was moments such as these that had the nation glowing with pride, underscoring the fact that true genius couldn't be repressed despite centuries of cultural and imperialist hegemony.

In this amazing turnaround, hundreds and thousands of Indians have played a key role. Selecting only few names has been an arduous task, with other equally deserving ones having been left out due to space constraints. his is not just a collection of achievements and milestones by select individuals – it is the story of an entire era.

I am grateful to M/s V&S Publishers for accepting this book for publication. Thanks also to Ms A Sunita Purushottaman for helping me in this endeavour. And grateful thanks to the editorial staff without whose untiring efforts this book would not have seen the light of day.

–Vishwamitra Sharma
C-3/58, Lawrence Road
Delhi – 110 035
Tel: 27194317

Poets and Writers

Rabindranath Tagore

Great Poet and Philosopher

(1861–1941)

Gurudev Rabindranath Tagore is one of our country's most distinguished and respected men of letters. Tagore was a novelist, playwright, painter, philosopher, educationist, freedom fighter and an actor. On 13 November 1913, he was awarded the Nobel Prize in Literature for his collection of well-known poems *Gitanjali*.

Tagore also wanted to evolve a world culture, a synthesis of eastern and western values, and towards this end he also founded an international educational institute Shantiniketan at Bolepur in West Bengal in 1901. Shantiniketan later developed into the Vishvabharati University.

Tagore was a voluminous writer. Besides the famous *Gitanjali*, his other well-known poetic works include *Sonar Tari, Puravi, The Cycle of the Spring, The Evening Songs*, and *The Morning Songs*. The names of some of his well-known novels are: *Gora, The Wreck, Raja Rani, Muktadhara, Raj Rishi, Ghare Baire, Nauka Dubi* and *Binodoni*. *Chitra* is his famous play in verse. *Kabuli Wallah* and *Kshudita Pashan* are two of his famous stories. All of us know that our National Anthem *Jana Gana Mana*... was composed by Tagore.

Rabindranath Tagore was born on 7 May 1861 in Calcutta. His father's name was Devendranath. The British Government honoured him with the title of 'Sir'. But he returned this title in 1919, in protest against the Jallianwala Bagh tragedy.

This great son of India died on 8 August 1941 at the age of 80. One of the last Century's most influential Indian authors, he was also an ardent nationalist who urged social reform.

Sharat Chandra Chatterjee

Litterateur with a Difference

(1876–1938)

The distinction of this famous and highly popular Bengali novelist is that he had the audacity to change the tradition of idealism that was created by Bengali literature. His works centred on the plight and position of women in society. Sharat Chandra Chatterjee was not born into a well-to-do family like Tagore, but with his exceptional flair for writing, he became popular as a great literary figure.

He portrayed the lives and times of people belonging to the lower strata of society who were oppressed, especially the womenfolk of Bengali society. An example of such a work is *Shrikant.* Whatever he wrote, he questioned the very ideals of the Bengali joint family system. He portrayed the society of his times with so much realism and emotion that prominent writers like Romain Rolland recognised him as a literary figure of the first order. That is why he became a popular writer within a short span of time.

Sharat Chandra was born at a village in Hooghly district of West Bengal in 1876. He was the second of nine children. His father had an interest in writing and handicrafts, but he could not pull himself together and work at one place. Sharat Chandra believed that he had inherited his father's 'restless soul'.

Having passed his matric from Bhagalpur, he took admission in Intermediate. But as he was not able to pay his fees on time, he was not allowed to sit for the examination. His mother's death and his father's scolding forced him to run away from home. Having wandered from home, he went to Calcutta and married a girl named Hrinmayi. He soon became a well-known figure in the literary circle of Calcutta. He published his first story in the form of a series in a magazine called *Yamuna*. Then he went to Hooghly and concentrated on his writing.

The female characters in Sharat Chandra's works have an air of mystery surrounding them and cast a spell in the minds of the readers. A few of his popular works are *Badi Didi, Parineeta, Panditji, Samaj ki Atyachaai, Chandranath, Shrikant, Devdas, Charitraheen, Grihadaah, Brahmin ki Beti, Path ki Devedaar, Shesh Prashna, Subhadra* and others. His prominent short stories are *Bindo ka Beta, Chhota Bhai, Ramer Sumati, Manjhili Didi,* etc. Sharat Chandra's works have been translated into almost all Indian languages. Many have also been translated into English.

Sharat Chandra Chatterjee died at the age of 62 after a long illness in Calcutta in 1938. There have been few literary giants in the 20th Century like him.

Premchand

Hindi Novelist and Short Story Writer

(1880–1936)

M unshi Premchand wrote in Urdu under his childhood name Dhanpat Rai, but it was when he wrote in Hindi that he became recognised. The one quality of his writing was that he gave a realistic account about the predicament of society. And this made him the *badshah* of Hindi novels.

Premchand was born Dhanpat Rai at Lamahi village in Benares (now Varanasi) on 31 July 1880. His father Ajayab Lal was employed as a clerk in a post office. His mother was Anandi Devi.

Premchand's early education was conducted in Urdu and Persian in Lamahi under the tutelage of a maulvi. He passed his tenth standard from Benares. When he was in the eighth standard, his mother passed away and when he was 15 years old, his father died. Then he had to face a lot of difficulties in life. He was appointed as a teacher at a school in Chunar on a monthly salary of Rs 18. He taught at various schools in Allahabad, Pratapgarh, Kanpur, Gorakhpur and other places. And while he was employed as a school inspector, he completed his graduation. While in Kanpur, he befriended the editor of *Zamana*, Munshi Dayanarayan Nigam, and published his first story in the form of a series in *Zamana*. His work *Prema* was published through Indian Press, Allahabad under the pseudonym 'Nawab Rai'.

The statement that behind every successful man is a woman holds good for Munshi Premchand. His first marriage was not a success. He later married a child-widow Shivani Devi. In spite of facing several hardships, she encouraged her husband to write. Many of his stories were written under the pseudonym 'Nawab Rai'. The first story that was published under his real name was

Bade Ghar ki Beti. The credit of introducing Premchand into Hindi literature goes to Mohan Dwivedi and Mahavir Prasad Poddar of Gorakhpur.

In the year 1917–18, he wrote *Sevasadana.* This was his first major Hindi novel. The novel depicted the problem of prostitution and moral corruption. His works portray the social evils of child marriages, the abuses of the British bureaucracy and exploitation of the rural peasantry by moneylenders and officials.

During that time, he was totally involved in the freedom struggle. He began to churn out articles that focused on social problems. So, he gave up his government job on 15 February 1921 and joined the Marwari school in Kanpur as headmaster.

In 1922, he returned to Benares and founded Saraswati Press. Along with *Gyanmandal,* he started writing for *Madhuri* and *Chand* magazines. The publication of *Rangbhoomi* (1924) exalted him to the status of *badshah* of Hindi novels. *Premashram* (1922), *Karmabhoomi* (1931) and *Godan* (1936) are the other popular works of Premchand. In March 1930, he brought out a magazine called *Hansh* but he was always short of finances.

He went to Bombay in 1935, wrote stories and dialogues for films, but returned to his native place the following year. He breathed his last on 8 October 1936.

'Jigar' Moradabadi

King of Urdu Ghazals

(1890–1960)

'Jigar' Moradabadi is considered to be one of the greatest Urdu poets. He wrote on various subjects and his compositions were simple but profound. His way of rendering poetry was so profound that poets still try to copy his style. He was not highly educated, but overcame these shortcomings.

With dishevelled hair, unshaven beard, bedraggled clothes and an equally intense stupor, before 'Jigar' turned to poetry, he sold spectacles at railway stations. Ali Sikander 'Jigar' Moradabadi was born in 1890 to Maulvi Ali 'Nazar', who was himself an accomplished poet. His father left Delhi and settled in Moradabad. Young 'Jigar' began composing poems at the age of 13. First his father and later 'Daag' Dehalvi, Munshi Amirulla 'Tasleem' and 'Rasa' Rampuri began to help improve his work. The influence of Sufism came into his work through the music of 'Asghar' Gondivi.

He had become an alcoholic, but one day took a solemn pledge not to touch liquor again and stood by it till the very end. But he became ill. Then he took to smoking, but gave it up later and took to playing cards. 'Jigar' Moradabadi had a good sense of humour and was a kind-hearted person. He was also a deeply religious person but kept away from religious fundamentalism. He protested against modernity but was influenced into writing progressive poems.

'Jigar' Moradabadi's first composition *Daag-e-Jigar* was published in 1921, then in 1923 a compilation *Shola-e-Tuur* was published by the Aligarh Muslim University. In 1958, he published *Aatish-e-gul* and the next year he received the Sahitya Akademi Award. On September 1960, the king of Urdu ghazals died in Gonda.

'Josh' Malihabadi

Eminent Revolutionary Poet

(1894–1983)

Thanks to his revolutionary poems, composed during the rule of the British, renowned Urdu poet 'Josh' Malihabadi was given the title *Shayar-e-Inquilab*. He had an incredible form of expression. His words were fiery and could inspire patriotism. After Partition, he moved to Pakistan because of which he was strongly condemned. But his poetry can never be forgotten.

'Josh' Malihabadi was born into a respectable family and had a great deal of sophistication. He was also fearless, brave and sentimental. In the poetry sessions where the audience consisted of Muslim clerics, he sang compositions which condemned them. When the audience comprised government officials, he sang the famous poem *Maatam-e-Azadi* and where women formed the audience, he sang *Hai Jawani, Hai Jawani*. Clergymen despised him, officials shunned him and women walked out in embarrassment, but 'Josh' remained indifferent.

'Josh' had a stout figure and a towering personality and would often mock and poke fun at others. Shabir Hussain Khan 'Josh' was born on 5 December 1894 in the family of a landlord at Malihabad town in Lucknow district, which is famous for mangoes. Even as a child he was temperamental. He would beat up children with a stick. As a youth, he become a fundamentalist and opposed family members. Later he renounced religious fundamentalism.

When the struggle for Independence was on, he became a part of the struggle and composed revolutionary poems. They were published, distributed and read away from public glare.

He went to Hyderabad to earn a livelihood, but could not. He then went to Delhi and started a monthly magazine *Kaleem*. After

Independence, Pt Nehru appointed him the editor of the Urdu edition of the monthly *Aajkal.*

In 1955, he was lured by some Pakistani leaders and shifted base to Pakistan. But the promises made to him were not kept and he lost the respect of the people too. Even in India, people rejected him.

In 1967, he retired and in 1983 he died a dejected man in Islamabad. In his autobiography, *Yaadon ki Baraat,* he praised India and Indian leaders lavishly. So the Pakistan Government confiscated the book. Around a dozen compilations of his poems have been published. How well had he said: "This is the rendition of a heartbroken man."

Harivansh Rai Bachchan

Most Popular Hindi Poet

(1907-2003)

A mong Hindi poets, perhaps nobody has gained more popularity than Harivansh Rai Bachchan – and the same popularity has been infused into his son, Amitabh, who has scaled new heights in the film industry. One can see the role of destiny here.

In the 1930s the publication of *Madhushala* saw him soar dizzy heights. In poetry sessions, the audience wished to hear Bachchan alone. With the publication of *Madhushala, Nisha Nimantran, Ekant Sangeet* and other compositions, he established himself as a prominent Indian poet. He began to be compared with other impressionist poets like Sumitranandan Pant, Mahadevi Verma, *et al.* In spite of being introspective, his poems occupy a special place because of the expressions, language and idiomatic phrases.

By writing his autobiography in four volumes, he established himself as a prose writer too. Thanks to his descriptions, his compositions were liked by people, but this caused many a controversy in the literary field.

Harivansh Rai Bachchan was born on 27 November 1907 at Allahabad, Uttar Pradesh. He graduated from the Allahabad University in 1929. It was during this time that he got married. He had completed his first year in MA in English literature when he plunged into the freedom struggle at the call of Gandhiji. For his livelihood, he joined the daily *Pioneer* that was being published from Allahabad. Soon he was appointed a teacher at Agrawal School. Those were testing times because his wife Shyamla was critically ill. In 1936, she died.

He then completed his MA second year. He continued with his poetic compositions and also found recognition. His compositions swept a Sikh teacher, Teji Suri, off her feet and she became attracted towards him. In 1942 they were married. Bachchan was then the lecturer of English at Allahabad University.

His second wife was his muse and infused new inspiration and life into Bachchan. Then his compositions *Halahal, Bengal ka Kal, Milan Yamini, Khadi ke Phool, Pranay Patrika, Aarti aur Angare,* etc. were published. In 1952, he went to Cambridge to carry on research on the Irish poet W.B. Yeats. He returned to India two years later with his doctorate degree. He worked at All India Radio for some time and then moved on to the Foreign Ministry in Delhi as a Special Officer of the Hindi language. Later he was appointed a Member of the Rajya Sabha.

Bachchan's poetic compositions span around three dozen. Besides introspective poems, he composed poetry in the modern technique. He has also translated some of Shakespeare's plays like *Macbeth, Othello, Hamlet,* and *King Lear* into Hindi and received rave reviews. For the translation of *64 Russian Poems,* he received the Soviet Land Nehru Award. He received the Sahitya Akademi Award for *Do Chattanen.* He was also honoured by the Afro-Asian Writers' Conference with the Lotus Award.

Bachchan was an invaluable asset to the literary world. His compositions are simple, which makes it easy for people to remember and hum them. His poems are the poetic depiction of the ancient experiences of the human mind and soul.

Poet Sumitranandan Pant said, "Had it not been for Bachchan, a very important and integral part of *Khari Boli* would have remained uneventful."

He died on 18 January 2003 in Mumbai.

'Agyeya'

Father of Modern Hindi Poetry

(1911–1987)

The credit of giving a modern touch to Hindi literature goes to 'Agyeya'. His poetry, stories and novels have not only established a new style, but have become a benchmark for contemporaries as well as for writers of the new generation. *Shekhar–Ek Jiwani*, published in two volumes, *Nadi ke Dweep* and *Apne-apne Ajnabi* are the only three novels that he wrote, but were enough to gain him recognition. About a dozen of his poems were also published, through which he gave a new direction to literature. The fresh appeal of his compositions was because of his language, expression and subjects.

His name was Sachchidananda Hirananda Vatsyayan. Apart from being a writer, he was also a revolutionary thinker, good editor and educationist and achieved fame in every sphere. He came under the influence of revolutionaries quite early in life. And so, he even spent time in prison. He worked as a bomb expert in Chandra Shekhar Azad's group, because he was the only person in the group with a science background. It was here that a litterateur was born and he wrote *Shekhar–Ek Jiwani*. He handed over the work to his sister while he was in jail. When the novel was published, it created ripples in literary circles. Thus began his literary career.

It was during his imprisonment in the jails of Delhi and Lahore that he began his literary and journalistic career. He worked at a weekly *Sainik* in Agra. Then he moved on to *Vishaal Bharat* in Calcutta. During the Second World War, he joined the army and looked after publicity and public relations. In 1946, he quit his job and took up writing. During this period, he had published a couple of poetry compilations. He adopted a new style of language and expression. He gave the name 'experimentalism' to his work. To bring together other poets of the same genre, he published the works of seven poets in a compilation called *Taar Saptak*. The compilation has found its special place in the literary field. Then he published *Doosra Saptak* and *Teesra Saptak* and much later *Chautha Saptak*.

Apart from writing, 'Agyeya' was also involved in teaching and editing. He was the guest-lecturer at California University and Germany's Heidelberg University. He was the editor of *The Times of India*'s weekly *Dinman* and the Hindi daily *Navbharat Times*. Besides, he also edited the monthlies *Prateek* and *Naya Prateek*. In the political field, he was a supporter of Jayprakash Narayan.

'Agyeya' was honoured with the Bharatiya Gyanpeeth and Sahitya Akademi Awards. He was awarded the Bharat-Bharati posthumously by the Uttar Pradesh Government.

Akhilan

Great Tamil Novelist

(1923–1988)

The greatest of all Tamil novelists PV Akhilandam received India's highest literary award, the Gyanpith Award, for his work *Chittarpave* (*Chitrapriya* in Hindi). He wrote over four dozen books and received the Sahitya Akademi, Soviet Land Nehru and other awards. He took active part in the freedom struggle and went to jail several times. He worked in the postal department and later in All India Radio as a producer.

Apart from writing stories and novels, Akhilan also wrote plays, essays and children's literature. Some of his works have also been made into movies. He wrote against social injustice in society. He led his life the Gandhian way.

The works of Akhilan like *Enge Pogirom* ("Where do we go?"), *Betri Tirunagar* ("Vijaynagar"), *Kayal Vishi, Airimalai* ("Volcano") and *Pavaivillakku* are popular. *Enge Pogirom* depicts the social, economic and political problems of the 6th Century. The protagonist is an educated prostitute. *Betri Tirunagar* and *Kayal Vishi* are historical novels. *Pavaivillakku* is an autobiographical novel.

Umashankar Joshi

Eminent Gujarati Poet

(1911–1989)

There is an extraordinary blend of realism and idealism in the compositions of eminent Gujarati poet Umashankar Joshi. Apart from the Sahitya Akademi Award, he also was honoured with the Gyanpith Award. He was appointed the vice-chancellor of Gujarat University and the chairman of the Sahitya Akademi.

Because of his Gandhian beliefs, he participated in the freedom struggle and was even imprisoned on a few occasions. With the purpose of preserving the ideals of Gandhiji, he composed *Vishwashanti*.

Among his published works, *Gangotri, Nisheeth, Pracheen, Aatithiya, Vasant Varsh, Mahaprasthan* and *Abhigya* are the prominent ones. He also translated *Shakuntalam* and *Uttarramcharit* and other Sanskrit works into Gujarati. He also wrote some plays. During his early life, he also wrote poems in English, but never got them published. He also edited the monthly *Sanskriti*. In 1976, he received the Gyanpith Award for his collection of poems titled *Nisheeth*.

The poet believed, "In the materialistic world when society becomes a target of insensitiveness and love loses its piety, man will find solace in poetry alone."

Salman Rushdie

Controversial Author

(Born 1947)

Salman Rushdie is a controversial English writer of Indian origin. He now resides in England. He has penned many novels. It was his third novel that raked up a lot of controversy. When *Satanic Verses* was published in 1988, Islamic fundamentalists claimed that the novel contained objectionable material that was damaging to the religion of Islam and Prophet Mohammad. Ayatollah Khomeini of Iran issued a fatwa against Rushdie and offered a prize of $6 million to the person who killed Rushdie. Since then, the author has been in hiding in England under the protection of Scotland Yard.

Rushdie continues to write and has written many stories and satirical novels. His other important works are *Midnight's Children* (1981) and *East-West* (1994).

Ahmed Salman Rushdie was born on 19 June 1947 in Bombay (now Mumbai). His father was a prosperous businessman. He studied at Rugby School and the University of Cambridge in England. After acquiring a post-graduate degree in history in 1968, he worked as a copywriter in an advertising agency. His first novel, *Grimus*, appeared in 1975. His second novel was *Midnight's Children*. It was about modern India. The novel earned him critical acclaim and international recognition. *Shame* was published in 1983. It mirrored the political life in Pakistan. It was *Satanic Verses* that created a furore in the Islamic world soon after its release in 1988.

Even while in hiding he continued to write. *Imaginary Homelands* was released in 1991. It is a collection of essays and criticism. *East-West* (1994) is a collection of short stories. Then came *The Moor's Last Sigh* (1995), *The Vintage Book of Indian Writing (1947-1997)* (1997) and *The Ground Beneath Her Feet* (1999).

In early 2000, when writers from the Commonwealth countries were felicitated in New Delhi, Rushdie came to India. When *Satanic Verses* was published and there were widespread protests, India had banned the book. So he appealed to the government to lift the ban on the book.

Salman Rushdie was born in Bombay but has lived abroad for many years now. His ancestral home is located near Solan in Himachal Pradesh.

R.K. Narayan

The Creator of Malgudi

(1906-2001)

Renowned English novelist of international fame, R.K. Narayan was born in Madras in 1906. He had his initial education in Madras (Chennai) and later at Maharaja's College in Mysore. He lived in Mysore, the place which had the most influence on him and was reflected in his novels, till his last years. Narayan travelled extensively. Most of his works, starting from his first novel, *Swami and His Friends* (1935) were set in the fictional town of Malgudi. His novels reflect Indian conditions and life and have a unique identity. Malgudi comes to life in his novel, leaving a feeling that the reader is part of Narayan's fictional place. Many scholars regard him as the greatest Indian writer in English and call him 'the Premchand of South India'.

Narayan started his career as a journalist in Mysore and later took to writing novels. He published numerous novels including *The Guide*, which was made into a Hindi film that went on to become a superhit. Most critics consider *The Guide* to be his magnum opus. It is a great romantic saga of a tourist guide and a dancer who meets him while on a visit to a hill resort with her husband.

He has published numerous novels (*Swami & Friends, The Dark Room, The English Teacher, Mr Sampath, The Financial Expert, Waiting for the Mahatma, The Vendor of Sweets, The Painter of Signs, A Tiger for Malgudi,* and *Talkative Man*); five collections of short stories (*A Horse and Two Goats, An Astrologer's Day, Lawley Road, Malgudi Days,* and *The Grandmother's Tale*); two travel books (*My Dateless Diary* and *The Emerald Route*); four collections of essays (*Next Sunday, Reluctant Guru, A Writer's Nightmare* and *A Story-Teller's World*); a memoir (*My Days*), and some translations of Indian epics and myths (*The Ramayana, The Mahabharata,* and *Gods, Demons and Others*).

In 1980, R.K. Narayan was awarded the A.C. Benson Award by the Royal Society of Literature and was made an Honorary Member of the American Academy and Institute of Arts and Letters. In 1989 he was made a member of the Rajya Sabha. He received the Sahitya Akademi Award for *The Guide* (1958).

R.K. Narayan's full name was Rasipuram Krishnaswami Ayyar Narayanaswami. In his early years he signed his name as R.K. Narayanaswami, but apparently at the time of publication of *Swami and Friends*, he shortened it to R.K. Narayan on Graham Greene's suggestion. He passed away in 2001.

Artists

Raja Ravi Varma

Eminent Artist

(1848–1906)

Raja Ravi Varma acts as a link between the 19th and the 20th centuries. He belonged to a period when Indian art form was trying to break away from the traditional mould and it was Raja Ravi Varma who cast it in the modern mould. His contribution to art is timeless and continues to cast its spell on art lovers even today. That his works still sell at exorbitant rates is proof enough that the charm and attraction of his paintings has not diminished with time. Many of today's painters try to copy his style.

Raja Ravi Varma was born on 29 April 1848 in Kilimanoor, some 36 km away from Trivandrum (now Thiruvananthapuram), the present capital of Kerala. He belonged to the royal family of Travancore. His uncle, Raja Raja Varma, was also a good artist. He taught the basics of painting to Raja Ravi Varma and later introduced him to the Tanjore style of painting. When he was 14, Maharaja Ayilyum Thirunal took him to Travancore and placed him under the tutelage of the royal painter, Rama Swamy Naidu. Three years later he started learning oil painting from a British painter, Theodore Jenson.

Raja Ravi Varma entered the field of art at the dawn of the Modern Age. Of the known artists, he was the first to work with oil. His works were greatly inspired by the European style. Rembrandt was his greatest inspiration, but the subjects of his works remained Indian goddesses and mythological figures. He was the first artist to adopt Western techniques and the principles of perspective and composition in Indian art. In 1873 he won the Governor's Gold Medal for his work *Nair Lady Doing Her Hair*. This made him a popular artist and the Indian nobility and Europeans in the country commissioned him to do their portraits. He did the portraits of the kings of Madras, Trivandrum, Baroda, Udaipur and other states.

He was also the first artist to put his works on display. Art lovers, collectors and many kings and maharajas had the opportunity to buy his works. This gave him an opportunity to move out of Kerala and interact with the people and culture of other parts of the country, and develop a truly national style in his paintings.

The portraits helped him gain instant success, but he moved to painting gods and goddesses from the rich Indian mythology. Some of his works where he captured dramatic and significant moments from Indian mythology include *Shakuntala's Love Letter*, *Vishwamitra-Menaka*, *Harishchandra in Distress*, *Sri Krishna–Balaram*, *Mohini*, *Rukmangada*, *Jatayu Vadha*, *Sri Rama Vanquishing the Sea* etc. The women depicted in Raja Ravi Varma's works are greatly appreciated. In fact the beauty of the Indian women is sometimes described thus: "She looked as if she had stepped out of a Ravi Varma canvas." It is truly a compliment to the great painter who successfully combined tradition with modernity.

It was in 1893 that his paintings were first exhibited outside Kerala and that too in Delhi. Till then, only kings, princes and the rich had the privilege of visiting a painting exhibition. Ravi Varma's paintings reached the common masses. This was an absolutely commendable achievement in the 20th Century.

To make copies of his originals by the lithography technique, he set up a printing press at a tourist spot in Lonavala in 1894. This resulted in further popularity of Raja Ravi Varma's paintings. His critics, however, condemned his works, pointing out that his paintings were only superficially Indian. They said that though he depicted characters and themes from Indian mythology, he was heavily influenced by Western styles of painting.

Some critics dismiss his works as calendar art, but his oeuvre continues to generate interest among art lovers even now. One of his paintings, *The Begum's Bath* once sold at a record price for an Indian artist.

Nandalal Bose

Great Painter

(1882–1966)

Nandalal Bose is known as the creator of painters because when Rabindranath Tagore brought him to Shantiniketan, he gave Bose the liberty to decide the curriculum of the students of art. As a result, Shantiniketan became a leading institution. It was Nandalal's prudence that was at work. He always tried to help the students get due recognition for their work.

Nandalal Bose was the president of Kala Bhavan of Shantiniketan. He was always concerned with the well-being of his students, so they called him 'Master Moshai'.

Nandalal Bose was born on 3 December 1882 at Munger in Kharagpur, West Bengal. His father worked on a canal project there, but was later transferred to Darbhanga region and appointed the sculptor of a school of architecture. As a child, Nandalal was not very interested in studies. While going to school, he used to watch the potters making clay toys. With the money meant for books and stationery, he bought books devoted to art. At the age of 23, he sought admission in Calcutta Arts School. There he met Abindranath Tagore. In the test Abindranath asked him to draw a picture of Lord Ganesha. Bose drew it with Tempora and watercolours. He passed the test and was taken in as a student.

Bose's paintings were inspired by the paintings of Ajanta and Ellora Caves. In 1910–11, he began to make replicas of the Ajanta paintings. As an instructor at Kala Bhavan, he earned recognition and fame. He accompanied Rabindranath Tagore on his tour to China and Japan in 1924. Among his famous paintings are *Sati, Kali, Alekshya Dasana, Swarna Kalash, Ardhnareshwar, Veenavadini* and *Parthasarathi.* He died on 16 April 1966.

Amrita Shergil

Maestro of Modern Art

(1913–1941)

A name to reckon with in the art circle, Amrita Shergil painted realistic art and became a well-known figure at a time when European painting was just in the initial stages. Besides she also portrayed Indian rural womenfolk with such natural beauty that her work was well recognised. In her brief life, she created such masterpieces that even decades after her death, her work remains much sought after. She started at a very young age and her work portrayed the talent of an inborn painter.

Amrita Shergil was the daughter of Umrao Singh Shergil of Majitha. She was born in Budapest, the capital city of Hungary. Her mother was a Hungarian. When Umrao Singh went to France, he made arrangements for his daughter's education in Paris. Her uncle, Indologist Ervin Batkay, noticed her talent early and encouraged her to paint. At 16 she entered a famous art school in Paris, Ecole des Beaux Arts. Here she was influenced by the works of Cezanne, Modigliani and Gaugin. The description she heard about India from her relatives invoked a desire to visit the country.

In 1921, she graduated in painting from the city of Florence in Italy. In the test, she painted a nude woman. For this, she was asked to leave the school. She had by this time realised that her sole ambition in life was to become an artist. So she returned to Paris and began to pursue her painting classes again. Soon the influence of Hungarian art in her works began to diminish and her inclination towards realism grew. Her works clearly showed this influence. Her famous paintings include *A Boy with an Apple*, and *Banana Vendor*, among others. The inspiration to paint Indian women came from her fans.

After coming over to India, she opened a studio in Shimla. She transformed herself in the Indian mould and began to paint with the Indian perspective in mind, gaining quick recognition. She wanted to invoke her Indian roots. In 1936, she toured the Ajanta and Ellora Caves and her paintings underwent a transformation. Instead of doing large paintings, she concentrated on doing small, realistic paintings. Thus, she gave a new direction to the Indian art scenario. She tried to fuse the aesthetics of the Ajanta and Ellora paintings with European oil painting techniques that she had learnt in Paris. Her style was a total contrast from the works of contemporaries like Abindranath Tagore, AR Chugtai and Nandalal Bose.

Many of her paintings have a peaceful and soulful expression. But in her own life, she was highly emotional as well as critical and abrasive by nature. Not many readers know that the nude paintings she did depicted reality. In one of her paintings, she portrayed two young girls in the nude, a common sight in rural India.

Her paintings showed diversity after she went on a tour to south India in 1937. This transformation can be seen in many of her works like *Brahmacharis, South Indians Going to the Market* and *Bride's Toilette*. Her work was different from the realist watercolour mode of Indian painting prevalent at the time. This makes it evident that Amrita Shergil's inclination was towards the depiction of modern India rather than being a part of the revival of ancient art that was taught at Shantiniketan.

In 1938 Shergil married a relative from her mother's side, Victor Egan, who was a doctor by profession. She stayed in a small village in northern India. She turned to seventeenth Century Mughal miniatures amalgamating their sense of composition and colour with the system she had developed from Ajanta oil paintings. But her life was cut short by the cruel hands of death. In 1941, at the young age of 28, she died in mysterious circumstances, having already achieved much recognition within a short span of time.

Maqbool Fida Husain

Controversial Contemporary Painter

(1915–2011)

Maqbool Fida Husain was born with a paint-brush in his mouth. He had said, "Even before I had outgrown my childhood, I was told by my father to earn my livelihood. In fact my first paint-brush was given to me by my father. I moved from Indore to Bombay... armed with a paint-brush in my hand and a passion for art... I just followed my passion and went with the flow."

His life was always embroiled in controversies. His works always remained controversial or high profile. He used extremely long brushes and paints. He was never embarrassed to exhibit his weakness for the fairer sex and was a great fan of Madhuri Dixit.

As per Husain, "I was not even two years old when I lost my mother. Maybe that is why my search for a mother figure is eternal... maybe that is the reason why, in most of my paintings, I never show faces. When I wanted to depict the affection of a mother, I painted Mother Teresa... the moment people saw that white saree with the blue border, they just knew it was Mother."

At one time he painted horses in full gallop. Could it be that the horses were symbolic of his restless and roving heart and mind? Apart from painting scenes from the *Ramayana* and the *Mahabharata* he had also drawn portraits of Mahatma Gandhi, Mother Teresa, Indira Gandhi, Amitabh Bachchan, Madhuri Dixit and Sachin Tendulkar. All these prove that an artist is always on the lookout for something new. He conducted his daughter's marriage ceremony in a chawl of a Mumbai suburb called Girgaon.

M.F. Husain was nominated to the Rajya Sabha for six years. He tried to portray society in his work. M.F. Husain was born on 17 September 1915 at Pandharpur in Maharashtra. After completing his initial studies in 1935 in Indore, he came over to Bombay to join the J.J. School of Arts. He began his career by painting cinema posters on hoardings. However, the money he earned was not enough to support him and his wife, Fazila, whom he married in 1941. Though he also tried his hand at designing toys and furniture, painting was his first love. He put up his first painting on display at the Bombay Art Society in 1947. It was titled *Sunhera Sansar*.

In 1948 on the invitation of the painter Francis Newton Souza, he became a member of the Progressive Artists Group. The group aimed at giving a natural expression to contemporary Indian art. There he was influenced by the German painter Emile Nolde and the Austrian Oscar Kokoschka, who were renowned painters of the Expressionist tradition. He was influenced by their style. In the 1950s he held solo exhibitions first in Zurich and later in Europe and the United States.

He joined hands with modernist architect Balkrishna V. Doshi and created the Husain-Doshi Gufa in Ahmedabad. It is a cave-like structure that knits diverse disciplines of art and architecture.

Husain was always inspired by cinema. His first work as a filmmaker was *Through the Eyes of a Painter*. It won the Golden Bear at the Berlin Film Festival in 1967. He depicted scenes from films like *Pather Panchali* and *Hum Aapke Hain Kaun*.

For his contribution towards art Husain was honoured with the Padma Shri in 1966, the Padma Bhushan in 1973 and the Padma Vibhushan in 1989.

Husain was indifferent to religion and politics and treated Hindu Gods & Goddesses with disdain depicting them unclothed and often in sexuality suggesting poses. This led to a series of cases as well as non-bailable warrant against him. Fearing for life, Husain left India in 2006 and lived in London & Doha. He acquired Qatari nationality. He expired on 9 June 2011.

M.S. Subbulakshmi

Melody Queen

(1916–2004)

Madurai Shanmugavadivu Subbulakshmi has the distinction of making it big in the field of Carnatic music when it was strictly a male domain. MS, as she is popularly called, was born in the temple town of Madurai, Tamil Nadu on 16 September 1916. Her mother Madurai Shanmugavadivu was an exceptional veena player. Young Subbulakshmi (the name means 'the auspicious goddess of wealth') grew up listening to the notes of the nagaswaram and the chants emanating from the Meenakshi Temple near her house. She dropped out of school when she was in the fourth standard and dedicated herself to music. Her guru was Semmangudi Srinivasa Iyer. Subbulakshmi was a child prodigy. She gave her first recital in 1926 when she was just 10 years old. She has continued to enthrall audiences since then.

In the field of music, India has produced many eminent musicians. And each occupies a special place in the music world. But what is it that puts MS Subbulakshmi apart? The answer is that as soon as she sets her hands on the mridangam, she forgets herself and words flow from her mouth and resonate in the air. The grace and dedication with which she sings has resulted in a huge fan following. She always wants her audience to be immersed in music and feel a divine presence.

In 1938, Subbulakshmi made her film debut with *Sevasadanam*. It was based on the theme of women's liberation. In 1940, she married Thyagarajan Sadasivam, a freedom fighter, who was also her guru and guide. A major credit for Subbulakshmi's success goes to her husband, who shaped her musical career. Sadasivam was also a filmmaker. Subbulakshmi appeared in Tamil films as a singing star, all of which were runaway successes. She acted in *Shakuntalai* in 1940, *Savitri* in 1941 and *Meera* in 1945. *Meera* was remade in Hindi and became a hit. The film made her a household name across the country.

However, it was her devotional songs (*bhajans* and *shlokas*) that made her truly famous in India and abroad. She has rendered her voice to the compositions of the Carnatic music trinity – Thyagaraja, Muthuswamy Dikshitar and Shyama Sastri. When she sang Gandhiji's favourite bhajan *Vaishnava Janato Tene Kahiye, Je Peer Parayee Jaane Re,* magic was created on stage and he was moved to tears. Amongst her famous renditions are *Shree Venkatesha Suprabhatam, Shree Vishnu Sahasranaman, Meera bhajans* and *Hanuman Chalisa.*

When MS sang at the United Nations Assembly, *New York Times* wrote that she could convey her message to Western people through her music. Although they could not understand the words, the sweet voice emanating from her throat made the message easy to grasp for foreigners. She also sang before the Queen of England at Royal Albert Hall in London.

When Sarojini Naidu heard her renditions, she said, "From today, I surrender to Subbulakshmi, the enchanting singer with an enchanting voice, my title (the Nightingale of India)."

In 1954 Subbulakshmi was honoured with the Padma Bhushan. She received the title of Sangeetha Kalanidhi in 1969. She was the first woman to be honoured by the Madras Music Academy. In 1974, she received the Magsaysay Award and the following year she received the Padma Vibhushan. She was the recipient of the Indira Gandhi Award for national integration in 1990. She was honoured with the Bharat Ratna in 1998, the first musician to be honoured with this award. She created a great void when her soul left for her heavenly abode on December 11, 2004.

Lata Mangeshkar

Greatest Female Playback Singer

(Born 1929)

There are a number of well-known playback singers in the music industry, but by rendering her voice to playback singing for film actresses, Lata Mangeshkar has not only helped them in finding a place of honour for themselves, but has also carved a niche for herself in the world of music.

Lata was the eldest child in a family of four girls – Lata, Asha, Usha and Meena and a brother, Hridaynath. Her father Dinanath Mangeshkar died when she was very young. She entered the film industry as a playback singer at the age of 13 in Marathi films. Nobody could have guessed then that the girl would go on to earn a name for herself and her family in Hindi playback singing.

On one occasion, she met Dilip Kumar. He told her that though a Marathi singer, she should pay attention to her diction in Hindi and Urdu too. And it did not take her long to establish herself.

The secret of her success is that she understands the story line of the film for which she has to playback. Then she studies the temperament of the heroine for whom she has to render her voice. When the film is screened, it seems that the heroine herself is doing the playback, not Lata Mangeshkar.

At a function when Lata sang the composition *Ae mere watan ke logon, zara aankh mein bharlo paani* by Pradeep for an audience that included prominent leaders like Pt Nehru, it brought tears to his eyes.

She has sung over 50,000 songs in 20 Indian languages for thre generations of heroines. This nightingale's velvety voice will continue to resonate for centuries to come. She had received the Dada Saheb Phalke Award in 1989. She was honoured with the Bharat Ratna in 2001.

Vallathol Narayan Menon

Poet & Patron of Kathakali & Mohiniattam

(1858–1958)

Vallathol Narayan Menon was an eminent Malayali poet. He is held in great reverence for his beautiful compositions. In recognition of his poetic talents, the British Government honoured him with an award in literature in 1923, but he displayed immense patriotism by refusing the award. The British Government was taken aback and insulted him by calling him a 'shameless Indian poet'. But this did not have any effect on the poet and he began his work with renewed vigour and vitality. He gave shape to various facets of the freedom struggle through his poetry. He believed it was necessary to keep a record of the past to help India on the path to progress. He felt it was difficult to sever ties with the past before proceeding towards the future.

His perception was very extensive. The contribution of Bala Saraswati, Rukmini Devi, MS Subbulakshmi, Ravi Shankar, Vallathol etc. towards art indicates a period of Renaissance of Indian art and literature. Apart from writing poetry, he also patronised Kathakali and Mohiniattam dance forms of Kerala. He set up the Kerala Kala Mandalam for the promotion of these dance forms. He toured the country and also went abroad.

Today both Kathakali and Mohiniattam have been given the status of classical dance.

Kamladevi Chattopadhyay

Reviver of Folk Arts

(1903–1988)

What is significant about Kamladevi Chattopadhyay is that she has made a contribution towards every field of art. Till Independence, Indian handicrafts were discouraged. Kamladevi organised the handicrafts sector, gave it the much-needed stability and tried to boost it. Her contribution towards handicrafts, music, theatre and dance is immense and incomparable.

Apart from handicrafts, ancient art forms like folk theatre, painting and singing have come down as part of our heritage. Due to colonisation by the British, proper attention was not paid to the ancient art forms and their survival was in peril. Another problem was the backwardness of rural women. In spite of being involved in handicrafts and folk art, their economic condition was very poor. When Kamladevi became a member of the women's wing of the All-India Congress Committee, she took important steps to improve the condition of womenfolk, though she herself was fighting heavy odds on the personal front.

She was married at a very young age and soon became a child widow. If she hadn't received the support of her mother and maternal grandmother, she would have ended up in a pitiable condition as hundreds of child widows did during that age. They were determined to give her higher education. She soon came in contact with Harindranath Chattopadhyay, brother of Sarojini, and showed interest in theatre. He wanted to marry Kamla, but he had to convince her and her mother. Kamladevi married on the condition that she be allowed to continue with her studies. Harindranath was able to instil a new lease of life in her.

Soon she began her work and strived not only to improve the lot of womenfolk, but society as a whole. She became an exponent of different forms of art and established a number of institutions for art and music. She was also the president of the Sangeet Natak Academy, and the vice president of the Indian Theatre Association and the Asian Theatre Institution. She was also the founder-member of the Handicrafts Board.

She started a number of training centres to provide special training for handicrafts. She also made provisions to sell the products made at these centres. It was because of her fine perception that the Central Cottage Industries could be established.

In the mid-50s, she was a symbol of art. She tried to give an artistic touch to Indian social life. Her contribution towards the field of handicrafts and Indian social life will never be forgotten. She received the Magsaysay Award in 1966.

Pt. Ravi Shankar

Renowned Sitarist

(Born 1920)

The contribution of Pt Ravi Shankar to the field of music will be remembered forever. There is no doubt that he plays magic on the sitar and has made instrumental music popular across the world. And that is what makes him incomparable. He has helped classical music and the sitar gain worldwide recognition.

It is because of his music that he is considered a world citizen. His students belong to different countries. Despite fame, he has never changed. He always wears a kurta-pyjama.

Pt Ravi Shankar developed the notation technique for teaching the sitar to his students. He has developed new tunes like *Parmeshwari, Kameshwari, Gangeshwari, Jogeshwari, Vairag Todi, Kaushiktodi, Mohankaunc Rasiya, Manmanjari, Pancham* etc. His compositions like *Vairagi* and *Natbhairav* are quite popular. It was Pt Ravi Shankar who composed the tune of *Sare Jahan Se Achcha*, and that too at the age of 25.

Pt Ravi Shankar was born in Benares (now Varanasi) on 7 April 1920. His elder brother Uday Shankar was a well-known dancer. Ravi Shankar toured the world along with Uday Shankar's dance troupe. He choreographed dance before taking to the sitar. At the age 18 he gave up dance.

For the next seven years he dedicated himself to gain command over the sitar. His guru was Allauddin Khan Saheb of Maihar. He worked as music director at the All India Radio from 1948 to 1956. Then he began to pursue his passion and undertook a series of European and American tours. He introduced Indian music to the west. George Harrison of the Beatles took up learning the sitar from him. Ravi Shankar has performed with renowned musicians and music conductors like violinist Yehudi Menuhin and symphony conductor Zubin Mehta. He even performed *jugalbandis* (duets) with tabla player Ustad Allah Rakha and sarod player Ali Akbar Khan.

Shankar composed a number of film songs like Satyajit Ray's Apu trilogy, *Meera*, *Godaan* and *Anuradha*. He composed *Raaga Swarna* on the occasion of the 50th anniversary of India's independence. In 1969 his autobiography *My Life, My Music* was published.

In a career spanning more than six decades, Ravi Shankar has been honoured with a number of awards. Various universities from India and abroad have honoured him with around 14 doctorates. He received the Padma Bhushan (1967), two Grammy awards (1966 and 1972), Padma Vibhushan (1981), the Magsaysay Award (1992), the Polar Music Prize (1998), Japan's Praemium Imperiale Award "for encouraging efforts of future generations of artistes", the Bharat Ratna (1999) and France's highest civilian award, Commandeur de La Legion d'Honneur (2000).

Rukmini Devi Arundale

Bharat Natyam Exponent

(1904–1986)

Rukmini Devi Arundale made an indispensable contribution towards art and culture. She is chiefly remembered for three prominent contributions in the field of art. Her marriage to George Arundale drew her close to ballet. It was then that renowned Russian ballerina Anna Pavlova advised her to find inspiration in the Indian art form.

Soon she was inclined towards Bharat Natyam. Till then this art form was practised only by the *Devadasis* – temple dancers who were looked down upon by high society. This ancient dance form was on the verge of decline. Then founder-member of the Madras Music Academy, E. Krishna Iyer inspired Rukmini Devi to take up the dance form. With the help of some motivated *devadasis*, she revived the declining art form. She gave Bharat Natyam a modern form by giving it a dress code, accessories and make-up, thereby imparting a permanent form to the dance. The worldwide recognition that Bharat Natyam has received is due to Rukmini Devi.

Though she belonged to a high-class Brahmin family, she learnt to perform on stage, inspiring ladies from a good family background to learn this dance form.

Another significant work of hers was the formation of Kalakshetra. The institution was run on the teacher-pupil tradition of ancient India. Art was being carried out through the centuries based on this tradition. Kalakshetra was established for the propagation of art and literature among the people and many famous artists and musicians have been associated with it.

She also started the tradition of musical dance ballets. She thus gave a modern touch to traditional dance and her contribution towards arts and culture will be remembered for ages to come.

Philosophers and Thinkers

Dr S. Radhakrishnan

Philosopher, Scholar and Statesman

(1888–1975)

Dr Sarvepalli Radhakrishnan is regarded as a unique amalgamation of an eminent philosopher and a national political leader. His interpretation of Indian philosophy in English has made people in the West change their perception about India. Dr Radhakrishnan is one of the few eminent personalities who had had a truly Indian upbringing and education. And he was able to make a mark in the Indian political, administrative, educational and spiritual spheres.

Dr Radhakrishnan was born on 5 September 1888 at Tiruttani, Tamil Nadu. His father, Veeraswami, was an astrologer and teacher. Dr Radhakrishnan received his early education from his father. He joined Christian College of Madras for his higher education. The one advantage he had of studying in a convent was that he got the opportunity to ponder over the Hindu religion. This was because the Hindu religion was criticised by missionaries. And this filled him with the desire to understand the true essence of Hinduism.

The speeches of Swami Vivekananda inspired him a lot. And that is why he did his post-graduation in philosophy. Then he worked at Presidency College, Madras till 1917. During those times, Dr Visvesvaraya was the diwan of Mysore. So at the behest of Dr Visvesvaraya, he joined Mysore College as a professor of philosophy. In spite of the presence of stalwarts like Dr Radhakumud Mukherjee and Professor Wadia, Dr Radhakrishnan became a popular figure in the university.

Dr Radhakrishnan did not obtain a doctorate degree. It was because of his competence, writing skills and insight into philosophy that many universities awarded him doctorate degrees. Just as Dr Visvesvaraya was keen to make Mysore an ideal state,

Sir Ashutosh Mukherjee wanted to promote Calcutta as a centre of science and education. So he invited Dr Radhakrishnan to Calcutta.

It was during this time that Andhra University was founded and he was appointed the vice-chancellor. He also had to look into the administration and organisation of the University. Although he joined Andhra University, he did not sever ties with Calcutta University. He was also given the financial charge of Andhra University. When he was in Calcutta, he was also associated with Oxford University, England. So he spent six months of a year in Calcutta and the other half in England. During those days, Madan Mohan Malaviya established Benares Hindu University and wanted to appoint Dr Radhakrishnan as the vice-chancellor of the University. Dr Radhakrishnan agreed to join as vice-chancellor but refused to work on a salary. In this way, he worked in Calcutta, Benares and Oxford Universities simultaneously. But when the work of Benares University required more of his involvement, he bade farewell to Calcutta University.

In 1942, when the freedom struggle took a new turn, the students of Benares University joined it. The British Government wanted to close the University. Because the students were also in favour of this, it would not have been difficult for the British to do so. But Dr Radhakrishnan was not in favour. Many considered this act of his unpatriotic, but it was not so. The institution founded by Madan Mohan Malaviya was a nationalist one.

Dr Radhakrishnan spent 40 years of his life as an educationist. Apart from being a teacher, he was also a writer, administrator and politician. His contribution as a teacher and educationist was noticed in Oxford, Calcutta and Benares Hindu Universities. Later, he was appointed the ambassador to the Soviet Union. And he was good at his work. It is said that when Dr Radhakrishnan completed his tenure as the ambassador and was taking leave from the dictator, Josef Stalin remarked, "You are the first person who treated me as a human being and not as a ghost. I am saddened by the fact that you are leaving us. I may not live long, but I wish you a long life." So saying, the mighty leader's eyes welled up with tears.

The diplomatic handling of the relationship between the two countries by Dr Radhakrishnan helped build friendly ties in the formative years of India's existence. What augmented the relationship was his humanitarian thought, simplicity and humanity.

When Dr Radhakrishnan returned to India in 1952, he was elected the vice-president. Between 1953 and 1962, he also served as the vice-chancellor of the University of Delhi.

On 11 May 1962, he succeeded Dr Rajendra Prasad as the President. The world welcomed his presidency. He always upheld the glory and honour of every post that he held. Be it as the Professor of Eastern Religions and Ethics at Oxford University between 1936 and 1952 or as the chairman of the United Nations Educational, Scientific and Cultural Organisation (UNESCO) between 1946 and 1952.

Dr Radhakrishnan was simple to the core. He always wore a *dhoti*, a *bandgala* coat and a turban. He tried to interpret Indian thought and philosophy for Westerners. His works include *Indian Philosophy, The Philosophy of the Upanishads, The Hindu View of Life, Eastern Religion and Western Thought* and *East and West: Some Reflections.*

Jiddu Krishnamurthi

Great Spiritual Thinker and Philosopher

(1895–1986)

Jiddu Krishnamurthi was born into a Tamilian Brahmin family on 11 May 1895 in Madanapalle, Tamil Nadu. His father was a government officer and when he moved on to Madras, he began to work for the Theosophical Society there. This was how the philosophy of the Theosophists influenced young Krishnamurthi. Seeing the exceptional qualities of the small boy, Annie Besant, the president of the Theosophical Society, proclaimed him as the incarnation of Christ in the west and the Buddha in the east. She took him under her wing and sent him to England, grooming him for his future role as the next world teacher. In 1911, an organisation called 'The Order of the Star in the East' was formed and young Krishnamurthi was appointed its head.

He spread the philosophy of the organisation around the world. He soon became world renowned and was accepted as one of the famous thinkers and philosophers of India. However, in 1922, he experienced a transformation in his ideologies. He questioned the basis of all philosophies and ideologies. In 1929, he dissolved the Order and returned all the money and property he received for his work.

Then he formulated a new philosophy after breaking away from the Theosophical Society. Krishnamurthi was a good orator and in a historic speech, he said, "I maintain that Truth is a pathless land and you cannot approach it through any path whatsoever, by any religion, by any sect." He believed that every person should strive to seek the Absolute Truth by himself. His teaching was: "You are the world and the world is from you."

Krishnamurthi travelled around the world and spread his thoughts to the people. He did not believe in any religion, philosophy or ideology. He believed that man could alleviate his sufferings only if he was determined to do so himself. He also believed that no religion, religious leader or guru could help in ameliorating the sufferings of mankind. It was for man to look inside and rid himself of fears.

He postulated, "To follow another in spiritual matters is to destroy oneself." He maintained that man should have a scientific bent of mind that is triggered by the religious spirit. And for this, man should have the right education.

After the death of Annie Besant, his association with the Theosophical Society was completely severed. Then he settled at California in the US. He died on 17 February 1986 in Ojai, California. A number of schools, beginning with the Rishi Valley School in 1928, were founded in India and abroad, especially in England and the US, based on Krishnamurthi's teachings.

Swami Chinmayananda

Spiritual Thinker

(1916–1993)

Swami Chinmayananda devoted his life to the spread of religious teachings of the sacred Indian texts, especially the *Bhagavad Gita*, the *Upanishads* and the *Vedas*. He also wrote around 30 books that attempt to interpret the dilemmas of the Hindu religion.

Swami Chinmayananda was born Balakrishna Menon on 8 May 1916 in Ernakulam, Kerala. He was born into an aristrocratic family of Kerala. After completing his school education in Kerala, he joined the Lucknow University for his Masters in English literature and law. In 1942, he took part in the freedom struggle and spent many months in jail.

After his graduation he joined *National Herald* in Delhi and wrote on varied subjects. Though he was successful in his profession, he was quite dissatisfied. The question of life and death and the futility of life and the role of spirituality haunted him.

It was then that he embarked on the quest for his answers. He undertook an extensive study of European and Indian philosophy. He was inspired by the writings of Swami Sivananda. In 1949 he became an ascetic and joined Swami Sivananda's ashram. He took the name Swami Chinmayananda Saraswati meaning 'the one who revels in the bliss of Pure Consciousness'. Under the tutelage of the Vedanta master Swami Tapovan, he studied the ancient Scriptures. He spent eight years here. It was then that it dawned on him that he should get across the message of the Vedanta to the people and bring about spiritual awakening in the country.

He conducted his first religious discourse (*jnana yagna*) in Pune. He soon carried it to prominent cities. The Brahmins (priestly class) were displeased by Swami Chinmayananda's method of open dissemination of the sacred knowledge of the Holy Scriptures. Till then the knowledge was restricted only to the Brahmins. Swami Chinmayananda put across the message of the Vedanta in a simple way that was easy for the common man to understand. He said that the Vedanta proposed to make man happier and contented in his daily life, leading to spiritual awakening from within.

He founded the Chinmaya Mission and preached the holy Indian texts. Every year he held a *Gyan Yagna* in one of the metropolitan cities. Apart from this, he also participated in social services and the spread of education and culture.

In September 1993 he went to Chicago to represent the Hindu religion at the Parliament of World Religions. He was the second Indian after Swami Vivekanand to be given the honour. He, however, suffered a massive heart attack and went into *mahasamadhi* in San Diego, California.

Swami Chinmayananda spent his life like a hermit of ancient India. Because of his selflessness and resoluteness, he was able to make the ancient Indian texts clearer and easy to understand.

Osho Rajneesh

Philosopher and Guru

(1932–1990)

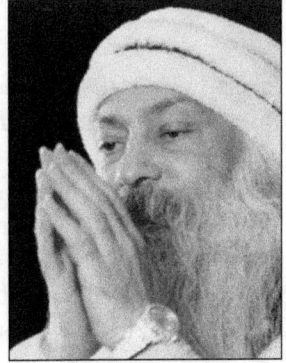

India is the home of many saints, philosophers and spiritual leaders. Many of them still influence society long after they are no more. Osho Rajneesh was one spiritual leader who tried to combine the thoughts and perceptions of Plato to early Chinese thinkers and modern philosophers. Rajneesh remained a controversial religious leader all his life, but there are thousands of his followers around the world.

The thoughts and lifestyle of Rajneesh were totally different vis-a-vis other spiritual leaders from India or abroad. Such people spend their life in meditation and in practising abstinence. But the ashrams and prayer halls of Rajneesh were no less than a modern discotheque. The more you unravel facts about him, the more amazing he seems. His spiritual world was established in the form of a discotheque-like ashram, a publications division, food larder and bakeries, all worth millions. The environment of his prayer halls was contrary to Indian culture. Rajneesh believed that man could achieve salvation only if he first got rid of his carnal desires and then concentrated on spiritualism. In his ashrams men and women were free to interact.

Even after examining his life and his spiritualism in retrospect, it is still not clear if he wanted to start a new faith or not. He has over 600 published books to spread his thoughts among the people and advocated a different method for the concentration of the mind, which is still followed by his followers. Rajneesh was severely criticised for his thoughts on sex and marriage. As a matter of fact, his life itself was surrounded by controversies. Yet he had over 500 prayer houses and meditation centres across the globe and they are still visited by his followers who meditate according to his interpretation of spiritualism.

Rajneesh or 'Osho', as he was later called, was born Chandra Mohan Jain at a village in Madhya Pradesh into the family of a Jain trader. After his education, he was appointed as a lecturer of philosophy at Jabalpur University. In 1966, he left his job and began to preach his thoughts. In 1970, he left for Bombay. There too he started preaching his thoughts in the evenings. Soon the number of his followers increased. Then he started a new form of renunciation and it soon became an international movement. He started his work with just six disciples. His objective was to transform his thoughts into an international one. In 1974, he came to Poona and established an ashram. Even after his death, the ashram continues to draw visitors and tourists. They come here to witness a unique phenomenon of prayer and devotion.

In India he was severely criticised for his thoughts and actions and so he went to America. There he bought 64,000 acres of land in Oregon and founded a city which was named Rajneeshpuram. The work in the city was carried out very fast. People were so influenced by his words that they donated their valuable possessions like Rolls Royce cars etc.

When the American Government perceived the emergence of a special type of culture which was in violation of immigration laws, it asked him to leave the country. Then he returned to Poona and died sometime later at the age of 58.

A controversial spiritual leader of the 20th Century, Osho has many followers in India and abroad. His thoughts and movement are kept alive by his disciples.

Sri Aurobindo

Prominent Revolutionary and Ascetic

(1872–1950)

There are some persons who act as a bridge between two periods, but there are some who cannot be bound within a period and leave their impression on the sands of time forever. The life of Sri Aurobindo is an example of such a person. Wherever he went, he left an indelible mark. His works and philosophy have not only inspired Indians but also the world.

It is sheer coincidence that he was born on 15 August 1872, the same day India gained independence some 75 years later. On the occasion of his 75th birthday, he gave a message which formed the dream of his life:

- There will be a period of renaissance in Asia and Asia will again act as a guiding light for human civilisation.

- India will be a spiritual guide for the rest of the world.

- There will be progress towards man's ultimate development and he will become capable of solving his problems himself.

Aurobindo Ghosh was the third son of Dr K.D. Ghosh and Swarnlata Devi. Influenced by Western culture, his father converted to Christianity. He had studied in England, so he sent his three sons to study at Loretto Convent in Darjeeling for their primary education. After two years, the father went to England and left his children at Manchester, where they studied at St Paul's School. Here Aurobindo studied English, French and Latin. At the age of 10, Aurobindo wrote poetry, which was published in *Fax Family Magazine*. Aurobindo took admission in King's College at Cambridge and also cleared the written examination of the Junior Civil Services, scoring highest marks in Latin and French.

A group of Indian students had formed a secret organisation called 'Lotus and Dagger' that worked clandestinely for the Indian freedom struggle. Aurobindo became a member of the organisation. He gave fiery speeches and recited patriotic songs at the congregation of Indian students called Indian Majlis in Cambridge. It was during these days that Maharaja Sayajirao of Baroda went to London and invited him to work in his kingdom. In 1893, he went to Baroda. His father died the same year. Aurobindo taught English and French to the maharaja. Later he became the principal of Maharaja College at Baroda.

After nearly 14 years in Baroda, he went to Calcutta in 1905, when Lord Curzon partitioned Bengal. Between 1902 and 1910 he strived vehemently to free the country from British rule. He made revolutionary ideas known to the people. He disagreed with the Congress policy of sending petitions and strongly supported the extremist wing of the Congress led by Bal Gangadhar Tilak. His association with the Congress in Calcutta for five years gave a lease of life to the party and it began to penetrate the grassroots level. But God had willed otherwise.

In 1910, when he went to prison, it dawned on him that his area of work lay elsewhere. Listening to the voice of his conscience and God, he forayed onto the path of spiritualism – which he considered the original gift of India to the world.

The British Government considered him a revolutionary. So to get away from the clutches of the British and to carry out his work without any obstacles, he went to the French colony of Chandranagar before moving on to Pondicherry, where he established an ashram for meditation and stayed there for the rest of his life.

According to Aurobindo, freeing man from the bonds of individuality would help mankind achieve *moksha* (salvation). He tried to bring about the union of different spiritual streams. He established a number of ashrams and founded Auroville along with a French lady Mira Richard, later known as 'the Mother'. Auroville is not just an ashram, it is a self-sufficient township, where people from all walks of life and different countries get a new life and work for the progress and betterment of mankind. Aurobindo died on 5 December 1950.

Film Personalities

Dadasaheb Phalke

Father of Indian Films

(1870–1944)

The Indian film industry is the biggest in the world. The number of films churned out by the Indian film industry in a year surpasses even that of Hollywood. Do you know who laid the foundation of the Indian film industry? It was all because of the earnest efforts of Dhundiraj Govind Phalke, fondly called Dadasaheb Phalke. He was inspired to make films when he saw a film on Christ. He dreamt of producing movies on Hindu gods and goddesses. And the realisation of that dream led to the formation of the world's largest film industry.

Dadasaheb Phalke was born on 30 April 1870 in Trymbakeshwar, Maharashtra. Even as a child he showed an inclination towards the creative arts. In 1885, he joined J.J. School of Arts in Bombay. He had varied interests. He worked briefly as a painter, a theatrical set designer and as a photographer in the State Archaeology Department. It was when he had an opportunity to work in the lithography press of celebrated painter Raja Ravi Varma that he was influenced by Varma's paintings of gods and goddesses.

In 1908, he set up Phalke's Art Printing and Engraving Works through a partnership. When it failed, it became difficult for him to make both ends meet. He also had to support his wife and children. It was during those difficult times that he saw the movie, *The Life of Christ* (1910) and his thinking and life took a dramatic turn. This happened during the Christmas of 1911, when he did not have the money or the knowledge about film-making. He arranged for the money by parting with his wife's jewellery, and made the trick film *Birth of a Pea Plant.* For this film, Phalke shot one frame a day to show the plant growing. He showed the film to Yashwant Nadkarni, a photographic equipment dealer, who was amazed by it and agreed to back Phalke. With this money, Phalke opened the Phalke Film Company.

All this took three years and in 1913 he made the film *Raja Harishchandra*. It was written, directed, produced and distributed by him. It is difficult to estimate the trials and tribulations he faced during the making of films. He learnt stage setting, photography, rules of theatre and even magic and illusion. He also mastered painting of the sets and designing as well as learnt the nuances of film distribution. This was indeed a pioneering effort!

In 1917, Phalke Film Company became Hindustan Film Company. He made around 40 films. At a time when films were considered taboo for women, he introduced an actress in the film *Bhasmasur Mohini* (1913). His other successful films include *Lanka Dahan* (1917), *Krishna Janma* (1918) and *Sairandari* (1920). In the 1930s when sound was introduced in Hindi cinema and the film industry expanded, he lost out. So he gave up film-making.

It was 25 years since *Raja Harishchandra* was made. When the Indian film industry was celebrating its silver jubilee, it failed to honour Dadasaheb Phalke. So he died a poor, embittered man on 16 February 1944 at Nasik. The Dadasaheb Phalke Award was constituted a year after his death by the government in recognition of his contribution to the Indian film industry.

Today getting the Dadasaheb Phalke Award for lifetime achievement is a matter of pride and honour for film producers, directors and actors. It is given by no less a personage than the President of India.

Madhubala

Enigmatic Beauty and Legendary Actress

(1933-1969)

Madhubala performed her roles with such flair and finesse that she always looked natural on screen. And this was what people liked about her. Even after the lapse of decades, her movies evoke the same response among the audience of today. She was a combination of beauty, grace and charm.

Madhubala's life was not a happy one. Madhubala's role in *Mughal-e-Azam* was highly appreciated. The character she portrayed in the film was similar to her plight in real life. She came from a poor family and the grace with which she faced the trials and tribulations of her life was similar to the ones faced by the heroine of the movie. She fell in love with her co-actor, Dilip Kumar and wanted to marry him. But her father was against the relationship because he would lose a goose that laid golden eggs. If she were to get married, there was none to take care of her 11 siblings.

At first it was difficult for Madhubala to secure permission to act in films. She came from an orthodox, conservative Muslim family and her father, Ataullah Khan, did not agree initially to let his beautiful daughter act in films. But Madhubala remained steadfast and her father had to give in because he had no other means of sustenance.

Her film career spanned just two decades from 1942 to 1962. She died at the age of 36, leaving behind a void which can never be filled. She started off as a child artist. Then she became a full-fledged actress and heroine with the film *Neelkamal* opposite Raj Kapoor. And then came *Amar, Mr and Mrs 55, Chalti Ka Naam Gaadi, Howrah Bridge, Kaalapani, Mahal, Mughal-e-Azam*, and others. In *Mahal*, she enchants us with the song *Aayega Aanewala*, in *Chalti Ka Naam Gaadi*, she charms us with her cherubic smile and grace as Kishore Kumar tries to persuade her to pay the fees of *Paanch Rupaiya Baarah Anna*, and she is at her best when she portrays herself as a desperate and defiant lover as she renders *Pyaar Kiya to Darna Kya* in *Mughal-e-Azam*.

She faced the vicissitudes of life with a smile on her face. Although she encountered a lot of agony and pain, she never reflected the same in her movies. She did her role in comedy movies like *Chalti Ka Naam Gaadi*, *Half Ticket* and *Mr and Mrs 55* with great poise and ease.

Madhubala is often compared with Marilyn Monroe of Hollywood. Both had great sex appeal, beauty, charm, and enigma. Both led unhappy lives and yearned for love. Both died young.

When she was denied permission to marry Dilip Kumar, she was heartbroken. Finally she married Kishore Kumar, but their marital life was cut short because of her untimely demise.

Durga Khote

First Actress

(1905–1991)

Durga Khote entered films when girls from good families did not work in films. But when Durga Khote, who belonged to a high-class Brahmin family and was educated, entered the film industry, she not only displayed fearlessness and sheer determination, but also opened the doors of Hindi cinema for girls from a good family background.

Before the entry of Durga Khote into films, female characters in films were played by men. When Dadasaheb Phalke made *Raja Harishchandra*, he wanted a lady to portray the role of Harishchandra's wife, Taramati. But as there were no heroines, he had to select a boy for the role. It was then that Durga Khote decided to enter films. In 1932, when V. Shantaram remade *Raja Harishchandra*, he cast Durga Khote as the heroine.

Durga Khote also did character roles. After *Raja Harishchandra*, V. Shantaram produced *Maya Machand* under the banner of Prabhat Studio and cast Durga Khote as a fearless warrior. She wore the clothes of a warrior, complete with a sword in hand and a helmet on the head. In one scene of the film, a character actor was attacked by an eagle. Durga Khote caught the bird and tried to control it till the trainers of the bird arrived. The role of Durga Khote inspired other actresses to take up such daring assignments. In 1936, Shantaram made *Amar Jyoti* in which Durga Khote played the role of a lady who is harassed and finally revolts against her tormentors.

Durga Khote exploded the myth that the film industry was not a place for women.

Satyajit Ray

World-renowned Director-Producer

(1921–1992)

In 1960 when Satyajit Ray returned to Calcutta, he seemed different from the crowd. Calcutta was the centre of Bengali culture and thought. Most people were influenced by Trotsky or Mao. What put Satyajit Ray apart were his thoughts and stature. At 6 feet 4 inches, he definitely stood apart.

Satyajit Ray was born on 2 May 1921 in Calcutta. In the beginning, Ray's interest was towards commercial arts because he was born into a family associated with arts and literature. His grandfather Upendra Kishore Ray was a writer and illustrator and wrote exciting stories for children. He was also the first to start a high-class printing press in Bengal. His father Sukumar Ray was a writer and illustrator of Bengali nonsense verse. So Satyajit Ray had inherited a rich legacy from his family.

However, his father died when he was just two years old. He was looked after by his mother. He studied in a government school where the medium of instruction was Bengali. In 1936, he joined Presidency College where he was taught English. In 1940, when he completed his graduation, he was fluent in both English and Bengali. At the insistence of his mother, he joined Shantiniketan, the university established by Rabindranath Tagore. It was here that he gained an insight into both Indian and Western culture, something which was to be tapped by him in his later life.

In 1943, he returned to Calcutta and joined J. Walter Thompson, a British-owned advertising agency, as an artist. In his 10-year stint at the agency he rose to the post of art director. He also worked for a publishing house as a commercial illustrator and soon became a leading typographer and book-jacket designer. His two typefaces – Ray Roman and Ray Bizarre – are internationally acclaimed. It was when he was illustrating the novel *Pather Panchali* by Bibhuti Bhushan Bandhopadhay that he toyed with the idea of converting the novel into a full-fledged movie. After working for some time in commercial arts, he went to London. There he had the opportunity to watch films made by contemporaries in Europe and America. It was then that he realised his true love was movies. He began to study and understand the nuances of film-making.

He was encouraged in the pursuit of his ambitions by French director Jean Renoir who was in Bengal to shoot for the film *The River*. The success of *The Bicycle Thief* (1948) by Vittorio De Sica with amateur actors, an offbeat story and minimal finances gave him the inspiration that he too could make movies.

As he was short of finances, he mortgaged his wife's jewellery. He continued with his job and in 1952 started shooting on weekends. In 1955 his movie *Pather Panchali* was released. People admired his work and the film. It received rave reviews from the people of Bengal and the West. The film won a major award at the 1956 Cannes International Film Festival. It is still rated one of the finest movies in the world. Then he made *Aparajita* (1956) and *Apur Sansar* (1959). The three films form a trilogy and revolve around a young boy named Apu who is in search of his identity. It symbolises the plight of an average Indian who is torn between tradition and modernity. In 1957, *Aparajita* won the Grand Prix Award at the Venice Film Festival.

Among his appreciated films are – *Jalsaghar* (1958), *Devi* (1960), *Teen Kanya* (1961), *Kanchenjunga* (1962), *Charulata* (1964), *Nayak* (1966), *Aranyer Din Ratri* (1970), *Ashani Sanket* (1973), *Jana Aranya* (1975), *Ganashatru* (1989), *Shakha-Prashakha* (1990) etc. He made a total of around 36 films. He also made two entertaining films for children – *Parash Pather* (1957) and the musical *Gopi Gyne Baga Byne* (1969), which was based on a story by his grandfather.

Besides being a film producer and director, he was also a good writer and editor. He revived the children's magazine *Sandesh*, which was started by his grandfather in 1913, and edited it till his death. His book *Our Films, Their Films* (1976) is a collection of his film-related articles. He has also written science fiction and detective novels. Among his well-known books are *Kale Aura Ajar*, *Kanchenjunga*, *Nayak* (dance ballets), and 12 stories.

Oxford University honoured him with a doctorate. He was the second film personality to receive the award after Charlie Chaplin. In 1967, for his contribution to journalism and literature, he was awarded the Magsaysay Award. In the year 1971, he was honoured with the Star of Yugoslavia award. No one in the film industry has scaled the heights that Satyajit Ray did in terms of eminence, popularity and artistic perfection. In 1985, on the occasion of the second centenary celebrations of the French Revolution, the then President of France, Francois Mitterrand went to Calcutta to present him with the Legion d'Honneur, the highest civilian award of France. As a rare gesture by the Academy of Motion Pictures, he was awarded a special Oscar for lifetime achievement. He was also honoured with the Bharat Ratna the same year.

In 1992, he battled for life for three months at a hospital in Calcutta before departing for his heavenly abode on 23 April. On this sad occasion, the then president said, "Just as the Hooghly River merges with the infinite ocean, Satyajit Ray's life has merged with infinite time. His use of the medium of cinema to spread tolerance is incomparable and will continue to remain so for times to come."

He is universally regarded as one of the three greatest film-makers of all time.

Prithviraj Kapoor

Legendary Film and Theatre Actor

(1906–1972)

With films like Sohrab Modi's *Sikandar* (1941), in which he played Alexander the Great and K. Asif's *Mughal-e-Azam* (1960), in which he played Akbar the Great, Prithviraj Kapoor proved that he was an actor par excellence. But very few people know that he was actually a theatre actor and excelled at that too. He began his acting career in theatres at Lyallpur and Peshawar.

He was the first to adopt a professional technique and attitude in Indian theatre. He named his experimental theatre, Prithvi. His fellow theatre actors say that in 16 years, Prithvi Theatre churned out 2,662 shows and he played the lead role in all of them. Even when he was ill, he was particular about doing his work properly. Holding a show regularly for 16 years is no mean achievement.

When Prithvi Theatre suffered from a serious financial crisis, he moved to films. And he soon became a famous actor too.

Prithviraj Kapoor was born at Peshawar, now in Pakistan. In 1927, after completing his studies, he joined Ardhesir Irani's Imperial Film Company as an extra and soon excelled as an actor. He acted in the first Indian talkie, *Alam Ara* (1931). His greatest asset was his powerful, booming voice. In the 1930s, he starred in many Hindi movies produced by New Theatre, a studio based in Calcutta, as the leading actor. Some of his successful films were *Rajrani Meera* (1932) directed by Debaki Bose, *Seeta* (1934) opposite Durga Khote and *Vidyapati* (1937) directed by Debaki Bose. In 1939, he went to Bombay and joined Chandulal Shah's Ranjit Movietone Company.

Despite his commitment to Hindi cinema, he was involved in the construction of Prithvi Theatre with the aim of promoting Hindi stage productions.

He was nominated twice to the Rajya Sabha. In 1969, he was honoured with the Padma Bhushan.

In spite of suffering from cancer, Prithviraj Kapoor continued to work. Among his last movies were *Awara* (1951) and *Kal, Aaj aur Kal* (1972), both directed by his son, Raj Kapoor and *Aasman Mahal*, directed by Khwaja Ahmed Abbas. *Kal, Aaj aur Kal* featured three generations of the Kapoor family.

Raj Kapoor

The Dream Merchant

(1924–1988)

Raj Kapoor believed that both politicians and film producers are performers. Both sell dreams. A politician sells dreams by promising a better tomorrow for the masses and a film producer sells dreams through his films. Raj Kapoor's films are proof that he never compromised on quality and sets for the sake of money. The production costs were heavy because he always wanted his films to fare well at the box office. His films were a reflection on Indian culture and people. The song *Mera Joota Hai Japani* ("My shoes are Japanese") indicates that though he accepted western culture and lifestyle to some extent, he was an Indian to the core – be it *Awara, Shri 420, Phir Subah Hogi,* and *Jis Desh Mein Ganga Behti Hai.* In films like *Sangam, Prem Rog, Satyam Shivam Sundaram* and *Ram Teri Ganga Maili* the chief protagonists were women who were true Indians to the core.

After watching his movies, film producer-director Kedar Sharma remarked that Raj Kapoor's portrayal of love on screen was like the raw passion of cave people. Film producer-director Mahesh Bhatt said that love scenes in Raj Kapoor's films were like the unsophisticated love of a schoolboy. Films like *Sangam* and *Prem Rog* cannot be classified under any genre. All his movies are timeless and evergreen, providing wholesome entertainment as well as a social message. *Aag, Barsaat, Awara, Shri 420* and *Jaagte Raho* are some of his memorable films.

Raj Kapoor started his career in the 1930s as a clapper-boy for Bombay Talkies and as an actor for Prithvi Theatre. Both the companies were owned by his father, Prithviraj Kapoor. He got his first major break as hero in 1948 with the release of *Aag,* which was also directed and produced by him. In 1950, he set up his own film studio – RK Studio. As a writer, producer and director, he made many films under the RK banner. In 1951 came *Awara* with the leading lady of most of his movies – Nargis. The pair became an instant success. His other notable films were *Barsaat* (1949), *Shri 420* (1955), *Jagte Raho* (1956) and *Mera Naam Joker* (1970).

People began to vie for roles under his banner and thought themselves privileged to be a part of RK films. He also made his heroines like Nargis, Vyjayanthimala, Zeenat Aman, Mandakini *et al.* famous.

Raj Kapoor is known as the showman of Indian films. For his contribution to the film industry, he was honoured with the Dadasaheb Phalke Award. However, during the felicitation ceremony on 2 May 1988 he suffered an acute asthmatic attack and collapsed. He died a month later.

Apart from being a great director, he was also a superb actor. People loved him in his portrayal of a naïve country bumpkin a la Charlie Chaplin.

Raj Kapoor was a fun-loving person. His films were full of life, vigour and passion. He wanted to sell dreams through his movies. He wanted people to forget their woes and go into a world of make-believe for a few hours by watching his movies.

Amitabh Bachchan

The One-man Industry

(Born 1942)

A mitabh Bachchan is known in the Indian film industry as the "angry young man". His genre of movies portrayed the hero as a protagonist who opposed those thoughts and beliefs that were harmful for society. His entry into the Hindi film industry gave a new dimension to Indian cinema and he was able to carve a niche for himself in the entertainment world.

When he came over to Bombay from Calcutta to join films, producers rejected him outright for his thin physique, long bamboo-like legs and baritone voice. Dejected, he thought of returning to the company where he was employed earlier.

It was during this period that he met Jaya Bhaduri (whom he later married) and other friends. Slowly, he started getting a few roles. He made his debut in the film *Saat Hindustani* in 1969, directed by Khwaja Ahmed Abbas. People noticed him after the commercial success of *Anand* (1970). It was Prakash Mehra's *Zanjeer*, however, which finally catapulted him to fame. *Zanjeer* was his 14th film and then there was no looking back.

In other films that followed, the genre of the "angry young man" continued. This not only influenced his male contemporaries, but also his female counterparts. It is because of this that in spite of having to compete with brilliant actors like Naseeruddin Shah, Sanjeev Kumar and Dilip Kumar, Amitabh Bachchan was able to rule the hearts and minds of the audience. With the image of the "angry young man", the down-trodden youth identified with him.

After *Zanjeer* came *Amar Akbar Anthony, Deewar, Sholay, Trishul, Muqaddar ka Sikandar, Kala Pathar, Shakti* and others. That he

71

was a versatile actor was proved by the success of his comedy movies like *Chupke Chupke* and *Namak Halal* and the romantic *Kabhi Kabhi.*

During the filming of *Khuda Gawah* in the mountainous terrain of Afghanistan, half of Afghanistan's air force was sent for the security of the film crew. Even the fundamentalist forces of Afghanistan were impressed by his portrayal of an Afghan.

Before entering films, he also did theatre and worked as a radio announcer for some time in All India Radio.

After *Shahenshah* in 1987 the Bachchan magic failed to light up the screen. But he delivered three hits in the 1990s – *Agneepath, Hum and Khuda Gawah.* Then he took a sabbatical from films. In the late 90s, he returned with *Mrityudaata, Lal Badshah, Bade Miyan Chhote Miyan, Major Saab, Kohraam* etc. None of them reproduced the old magic.

Amitabh Bachchan was born on 11 October, 1942 at Allahabad, Uttar Pradesh. His father, poet Harivansh Rai Bachchan and mother, Teji Bachchan were advocates of modern thinking. During Rajiv Gandhi's tenure as prime minister, Amitabh Bachchan was elected to the Lok Sabha from the Allahabad constituency.

In the year 2000, after he hosted the TV programme *Kaun Banega Crorepati,* Star TV catapulted to the No. 1 slot, dethroning Zee TV. His entry into television changed the rules of the game, disproving the critics' contentions. In a poll survey on BBC, Amitabh Bachchan was named the Star of the Millennium beating top Hollywood legends like Charlie Chaplin, Sir Laurence Olivier *et al.*

His son Abhishek Bachchan married the top film star Aishwarya Rai on 20 April 2007. The couple has a daughter.

Currently he is busy hosting a TV show 'Kaun Banega Crorepati V' in 2011 besides acting in Bollywood and Foreign Films including one actor namely De Caprio of 'Titanic' fame.

M.G. Ramachandran

The Filmi Deity

(1917–1987)

Marathur Gopala Ramachandran was born in Kandy, Sri Lanka. Later his family moved to Tamil Nadu where they lived in poverty. At the age of 6, he joined a theatre group – the Madurai Original Boys – where he learnt acting, dancing and swordplay.

MGR made his screen debut in *Sati Leelavathi* (1936) but his first major breakthrough came with *Rajakumari* (1947). MGR's 1950s screen persona in adventure films constructed an image of political as well as physical invincibility. Often the themes of his films were derived from heroic ballads, which are part of the oral tradition of rural Tamil Nadu. For example, *Madurai Veeran* (1956), one of his most popular films, is based on the legend of Madurai Veeran, a popular deity of southern Tamil Nadu.

In the 1960s MGR turned to more 'realistic' fantasies, mostly in a contemporary setting, often playing someone from the oppressed class – a peasant, taxi driver or fisherman. For millions of fans, his image as the knight in shining armour, saving damsels in distress and being totally dutiful towards his mother, was a reality. He based his popularity on love and respect for the mother tongue, motherland and motherhood. He was considered the champion of lower castes/classes who repelled against their exploitation by the upper castes/classes – in reel and real life.

In *Engal Thangam* (1970) for example, playing a truck driver Thangam, MGR fights, sings, cares for the poor and preaches against smoking and drinking.

MGR's stint in politics was equally successful. He had joined the DMK party in 1953 and remained its member till 1972. He fell out with the DMK chief Karunanidhi and used the DMK's propaganda idiom against the DMK itself in *Nam Naadu*. In 1972, he set up the rival Anna-DMK party. In 1977 his party, renamed the AIADMK, won the state elections in alliance with the Congress (I). MGR became the chief minister of Tamil Nadu and was re-elected for three consecutive terms. He introduced several populist schemes like a mid-day meal for school children.

He survived a bullet wound when shot by fellow actor M.R. Radha in 1967. Despite suffering a paralytic stroke in 1984, he survived for three years.

He was awarded the Bharat Ratna in 1988 (posthumously). When he died in 1987, his funeral procession comprised over two million people!

A temple has been built in Madras with MGR as the deity.

Dilip Kumar

The Tragedy King

(Born 1922)

Dilip Kumar was born Yusuf Khan at Peshawar (now in Pakistan) into an orthodox middle-class Muslim family. Later, his family moved to Bombay in search of a livelihood. After the initial struggle, he was introduced into the world of arc lights and grease paint by the prime actress of those times, Devika Rani. Following his debut in *Jwar Bhata* in 1944, he played a variety of characters during a tremendously successful career of over six decades.

Critics hail him as the monarch of tragedy for his popular portrayal of characters subjected to unhappiness, misfortune and loss of loved ones. In *Devdas* he plays the tragic role of a young man madly in love with a woman who is married to another man. He loses his beloved and follows the path of self-destruction. He continues to love and adore her till his very end. With Raj Kapoor and Dev Anand, he formed the famous star trinity of the 1950s backed by the success of films such as *Andaz, Aan, Daag, Madhumati, Ganga Jamuna* and *Ram Aur Shyam.* His performances in the tragical dramas *Deedar* and *Devdas* are often regarded as the epitome of emoting. He was awarded the Filmfare Best Actor Award eight times. He won it for the first time in 1953 for *Daag,* in 1955 for *Azaad,* in 1956 for *Devdas,* in 1957 for *Naya Daur,* in 1960 for *Kohinoor,* in 1964 for *Leader,* in 1967 for *Ram Aur Shyam* and in 1982 for *Shakti.* He produced only one film in which he acted too. This film, *Ganga Jamuna* (1958), became an all-time hit and won many awards. He is the proud recipient of the Dadasaheb Phalke Award.

The doyen of Hindi films, Dilip Kumar is regarded by many as the greatest actor of Indian cinema and as an institution in acting. He has inspired and influenced many actors of his age.

Till today, many actors idolise him and imitate his style of acting and dialogue delivery. But few have been able to create the same magic on the silver screen, as he did. He played memorable character roles in films like *Vidhata*, *Shakti*, *Karma* and *Saudagar*.

He created a hit romantic pair with Madhubala – in real and reel life; the crowning glory being *Mughal-e-Azam* in which he played the role of a besotted Salim. This film became a superhit and created many box-office records.

In recognition of his contribution to the field of entertainment, he was nominated a member of the Rajya Sabha by the Government of India. Today, he is leading a happy retired life with his wife Saira Bano – a leading actress of her time.

Meena Kumari

The Tragedy Queen

(1933–1972)

Meena Kumari was born Mahajabeen in 1933 into an orthodox, lower middle-class Muslim family. She was the second of three daughters of Alibux and Prabhawati. In order to support the large family, she had to work as a child-actress. With *Leather Face* (1939), she began her filmi career at the age of six.

In *Baiju Bawra*, she was given her screen name Meena Kumari. Playing Baiju's self-sacrificing sweetheart Gauri, she won accolades for her captivating expressions while singing *Tu Ganga ki mauj main Jamuna ka dhara* with Bharat Bhushan and then as Baiju's lovelorn beloved crooning *Mohe bhool gaye sanwariya*. With the super success of *Baiju Bawra* she climbed to dizzy heights of fame. In Kamal Amrohi's *Daera*, Meena played Sheetal, a 16-year-old girl given in marriage to an old, ailing man often mistaken for her father. The anguish and agony on her face was heart-rending. She was pearless in expressing emotional turmoils and tribulations of the character she played on screen. Some of her films like *Phool aur Patthar* and *Pakeezah* were big budget films that are among the all-time greats.

A role she played to near-perfection was in the Guru Dutt classic *Sahib Bibi aur Ghulam* (1962), as the *chhoti bahu*. In this film, she rebels against the social and religious milieu, resorts to alcohol and dance and desperately tries to seduce her husband, so that he might remain faithful. The scenes and songs of the film like *Na jao saiyan, chhuda ke bahiyan...* shall ever remain etched in the memories of cine lovers.

Earlier in Bimal Roy's *Parineeta* (1953) too, Meena had played a similar role. She was a blend of devotion, pain and purity on the screen. In *Bhabhi ki Chudiyan* she spends her life and even relinquishes it in catering to the emotional and physical demands of her family. This image is repeated in *Dushman* (1971) and Gulzar's *Mere Apne* (1971), although with an emphasis on righteousness. In the latter, the mother-figure weaves her cleansing magic.

However, her crowning glory came with *Pakeezah* (1972), an immortal film about a virginal dancing girl who maintained her intrinsic chastity despite catching the fancy of all the Nawabs and the nouveau riche of the city.

She was known for romantic liaisons with her co-stars. Meena Kumari was the first recipient of the Filmfare Best Actress Award for the film *Baiju Bawra* (1953) and received it four times in all.

Released in February 1972, *Pakeezah* opened to a lukewarm response but after her death on 31 March 1972, the film went on to become a huge success and has since then acquired a legendary status.

Sporting Legends

Dhyan Chand

Outstanding Hockey Player

(1906–1979)

D hyan Chand wrote in his autobiography, "It's important all of you realise that I am just an ordinary man." This speaks volumes about his greatness, but also depicts his frustration. It is not surprising that these words should come from someone who led the Indian hockey team and won the first Olympic gold medal in 1928 for India. After achieving this honour for India, he advised his son not to take up the sport as it offered nothing in return.

Dhyan Chand joined the Indian Army as an ordinary soldier and in 1926, after a tour of New Zealand, he was promoted to the post of Lance Nayak. After the 1936 Berlin Olympics, he became a world renowned figure, but on the personal front, he gained nothing from all this publicity.

He wrote in his autobiography *Goal*: "After the tour of New Zealand, I became a household name. I thought I was very lucky, but my illusion was brought to a cruel end when I went to the 1936 Berlin Olympics as captain of the Indian hockey team. I saw that if any German soldier performed well, he would be promoted to the post of lieutenant the very next day. Taking that into consideration, I am sure that Hitler would have made me his Field Marshal."

Dhyan Chand represented India in three Olympic Games – 1928 Amsterdam, 1932 Los Angeles and the 1936 Berlin Olympics. Seeing him play and score goals, it seemed that he held a magic wand. In the 37 matches played, India scored 338 goals out of which Dhyan Chand alone scored 133. In his next tour to New Zealand, he scored 201 goals in 43 matches. The 1936 Berlin Olympics was a memorable moment both for India and

Dhyan Chand. India reached the finals after defeating Hungary 4-0, USA 7-0, Japan 9-0, and France 10-0. In the finals, India defeated Germany 8-1.

There were many myths associated with Dhyan Chand and his game. Some believed that his hockey stick had a magnet, which attracted the ball and helped him score goals. Actually, Dhyan Chand had an inborn talent. He could judge and analyse the next move of players of the opposite team just as a skilled chess grandmaster anticipates the moves of his opponents and plays accordingly.

He was conferred the Padma Bhushan in 1956.

Sunil Gavaskar

Outstanding Opening Batsman

(Born 1949)

Sunil Manohar Gavaskar was one of the most outstanding openers in the history of Test cricket. In 1971, he was selected for the West Indies tour. He amassed 774 runs at an average of 154.80 on the tour. India defeated West Indies and later, England. In 1976, India defeated New Zealand and in 1978, Australia, on their home ground. India emerged victorious in all these matches because of the splendid performances by Gavaskar. The 1971 victory was the first away from home after 40 years. In a career spanning 16 years, Sunil Gavaskar captained the Indian team in 46 Test matches.

Sunil Manohar Gavaskar was born on 10 July 1949. He started playing under the guidance of his uncle Madhav Mantri, who was himself a Test-playing cricketer. He was nicknamed "Little Master" for his short stature.

He holds the record for the most centuries – 34, of which 16 were scored against the formidable West Indies. This is an amazing record. He took 100 catches too. He is the only Indian to have scored two centuries in a Test match thrice. He was also the first player to score 10,000 runs in Test cricket.

What is special about Sunil Gavaskar is that he displayed a great deal of strength and stability while playing the game. He also infused his team with confidence.

After his retirement from cricket, he writes columns in newspapers and works as a commentator on TV. After proving himself in the game of cricket, he has now earned fame as a cricket columnist and commentator.

P.T. Usha

Sprint Queen of India

(Born 1964)

Usha's name is a force to reckon with because she practised hurdles by jumping over the walls of her house and broke into the field of athletics, which was then a male bastion. In fact, the credit of inspiring other women to take up sports goes to P.T. Usha. She had her first brush with success and fame at the 1982 Asian Games held in New Delhi, where she won two silver medals.

However, success eluded her at the 1984 Los Angeles Olympics, where she failed to secure the bronze by one-hundredth of a second. She was the first Indian woman to reach the finals of an Olympic event. Although she finished fourth, she set an Asian record of 55.42 seconds for the 400m hurdles. In the Asian Track and Field Championships held at Djakarta, Indonesia in 1985, she won the 100m, 200m, 400m, 400m hurdles and 4 × 400m relay. The record of winning five golds in a single international meet earned her the title of 'India's Golden Girl'.

At the X Asian Games held in Seoul in 1986, she again shot into prominence. She won the 200m in 23.44 secs, 400m in 52.16 secs and 400m hurdles in 56.06 secs. She also earned a name for herself in the 4 × 400m relay race. After the Seoul Asian Games, she returned home with four gold and one silver medals. In the Asian Track and Field Meet held in 1989, she was adjudged the best female athlete.

In spite of putting up a good performance at the Olympics, like Milkha Singh, she was not able to win any medals. But she became a source of inspiration to other women athletes.

Pilavullakandi Thekkeparambil Usha, or simply P.T. Usha, was born at a seaside village called Payolli in Kerala on

27 June 1964. The little girl loved to run on the beach. At the age of 13, Usha joined the government-run sports school at Cannanore. It was here that O.P. Nambiar spotted her potential and took her under his wing.

After marriage in 1991, she discontinued participation in sports for three years. Encouraged by her husband, when she returned to the arena in 1994 to compete as a veteran at the Asian Track and Field Event held in Japan in 1998, she won two bronze medals. She has till now won 102 international medals. At the Asian Games held in Japan, she won two medals. She has thus proved that marriage has not dampened her spirit to succeed in the game.

P.T. Usha was awarded the Padma Shri in 1984 and also received the Arjuna Award in the same year.

Viswanathan Anand

Chess Grandmaster

(Born 1969)

Viswanathan Anand is one player who has strived on his own to put India on the international chess scene. He became a grandmaster at the age of 17. At the age of 27, he became the world's number 2 chess grandmaster.

Anand was introduced to the game at the age of six by his mother. Born on 11 December 1969 in Madras (now Chennai), Anand soon learnt the nuances of the game and was nicknamed "the lightning kid" for his quick moves. At the age of 14, he won the National Sub-Juniors Championship. In 1987, he won the World Junior Championship in Philippines. The following year he was awarded the grandmaster title – the first Indian to achieve this. In 1997 he was awarded the Chess Oscar. In 1999 he was ranked world number two, second only to Garry Kasparov. He was the second non-Russian to come close to winning the title after Bobby Fisher in 1972. He once said, "I play chess to win, but more importantly because I love the game."

In recognition of his outstanding performances, the government conferred the Arjuna Award in 1985, the Padma Shri in 1988, and the Padma Bhushan in 2000. Padma Vibhushan, the second highest civilian award in India was awarded to him in 2007. He wrote a book, *My Best Games of Chess*, a collection of 40 of his best games. It received the 'Book of the Year Award' in 1998 from the British Chess Federation.

Anand won the FIDE world chess championship in 2000 for the first time; and was joint 2nd in 2005. He again won the world chess championship in 2007 (Mexico City, Mexico), in 2008 (in Bonn, Germany), in 2010 (Sofia, Bulgaria) and in 2012 will defend his title in Moscow (Russia) against Boris Gelfand, the winner of candidates matches 2011.

Success and titles have not made him proud or arrogant. He is very polite and humble and personally attends to the e-mails sent by ardent fans.

Sachin Tendulkar

Master Blaster

(Born 1973)

Sachin Tendulkar was just on the threshold of manhood when the world began to compare him with the greatest Australian cricketer Sir Donald Bradman.

Sachin Ramesh Tendulkar was born on 24 April 1973. He learnt the nuances of the game from his coach, Ramakant Achrekar, at a very young age. He made his debut at the age of 16 in Pakistan in 1989 – the youngest player to play Test and one-day cricket. He surpassed many records of batting wizards like Sunil Gavaskar, Vivian Richards, Javed Miandad and others.

Sir Donald Bradman paid the highest tribute to him when he said that among all the players who played international cricket in the past 50 years, it was Sachin Tendulkar who came the closest to his batting style. The records he has established rank him as one of the greatest batsmen of the game. Indeed, *Wisden* (the Bible of cricket) has rated him the second best batsman of all time in Test cricket (after Don Bradman) and one-day cricket. Until now he has scored 51 centuries in Test cricket, beating the record of 34 Test centuries by Sunil Gavaskar, and 48 centuries in one-day international matches. He is the only player to score a double Century in one day internationals.

Apart from being a good batsman, he is also a good bowler and is known to break batting partnerships. The fact is that Tendulkar's game is both impressive and incomparable. When he is on the field, millions of Indians wait with bated breath. He has received countless awards, honours, prize money and cars.

Sachin Tendulkar, to date has amassed more than 15000 runs in Test Cricket and 18000 runs in one-day internationals.

Mihir Sen

Champion Swimmer

(1930–1997)

What Mihir Sen achieved in his time in international swimming is significant, although the records he created have been subsequently bettered. In 1966, he established five important records and became an extraordinary salt-water swimmer. He was the first Asian to have crossed the English Channel. In 1959, he was awarded the Padma Shri and in 1967 the Padma Bhushan.

In 1958, Mihir Sen swam across the English Channel. In 1966, he crossed the Palk Strait, followed by the Strait of Gibraltar, the Bosporus Canal and the Panama Canal. Thus, he established records in long-distance swimming.

Mihir Sen was born on 16 November 1930 in Purulia (West Bengal). He was a lawyer by profession, a barrister of the Calcutta High Court. He was a peerless swimmer, having swum more than 600 kilometres in sea/ocean water. He brought glory to his motherland by creating records and earning a place in *The Guinness Book of World Record*. He died in 1997 after a brief illness.

Kapil Dev

Outstanding All-Rounder

(Born 1959)

Kapil Dev has been India's finest all-rounder in cricket. On January 30 1994, he became the most successful bowler with 431 wickets after the Bangalore Test against Sri Lanka. With this, he equalled the world record of New Zealand's Sir Richard Hadlee who too has 431 wickets to his credit.

When Kapil Dev was just 20, he set a new record of scoring 1,000 runs and taking 100 wickets. He made this record within a period of one year and 109 days only. He started playing first-class cricket in 1975. The opportunity to play in a Test match for the first time came in 1978, during India's tour to Pakistan. The main credit for India's victory at the 1983 World Cup in England goes to Kapil Dev. He was recently honoured with the Wisden Indian Cricketer of the Century Award.

Kapil Dev Nikhanj was born on 6 January 1959 in Haryana. His family dealt in the timber business and later settled in Chandigarh. Kapil Dev did not play cricket until he was 13. He got a break when his name was included in the Sector 16 cricket team as a substitute. Kapil Dev has written his autobiography titled *By God's Decree.*

He has achieved the unique feat of scoring 5,226 runs and taking 434 wickets in 131 Test matches, the first-ever Indian player to do so. He has since retired from professional cricket. Although his name was cited in the match-fixing controversy, he came out unscathed, as the charges could not be substantiated.

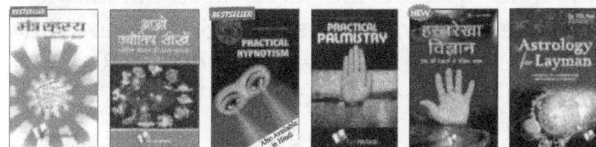

HINDI LITERATURE

TALES & STORIES

MUSIC/MYSTERIES/MAGIC & FACT

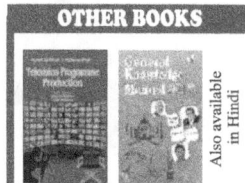

All Books Fully Coloured

Also Available in Hindi

OTHER BOOKS

Also available in Hindi

CHILDREN TALES (बच्चों की कहानियाँ)

BANGLA LANGUAGE (बांग्ला भाषा)

All books available at www.vspublishers.com

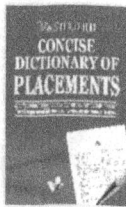
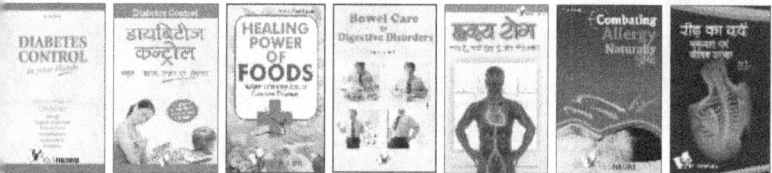